GETTING UNDER WAY:

NEW AND SELECTED POEMS

BY COLETTE INEZ

STORY LINE PRESS
1993

ISBN: 0-934257-59-0 cloth
ISBN: 0-934257-60-4 paper

Book design by Lysa McDowell

Published by Story Line Press, Inc., Three Oaks Farm in Brownsville, OR 97327

This publication was made possible thanks in part to the generous support of the Nicholas Roerich Museum, the Andrew W. Mellon Foundation, and our individual contributors.

ACKNOWLEDGEMENTS

I would like to thank Charlotte Mandel and Pamela "Jody" Stewart for their encouragement and good advice in revising some of these poems. I am also much indebted to a fellowship from the Guggenheim Foundation, the National Endowment for the Arts and to residencies at Yaddo, the Djerassi Foundation, the Virginia Center for the Creative Arts, Blue Mountain Center and the Millay Colony for the Arts, places which generously provided me with time for writing and editing a number of these poems. And my deep gratitude to Bucknell Universtiy for my post as poet-in-residence at the Stadler Center for Poetry.

Poems from the following collections are reprinted by permission of the author: *The Woman Who Loved Worms*, ©1972, Doubleday & Company, Inc., New York, NY; and, *Alive and Taking Names*, ©1977, Ohio University Press, Athens, OH. Selections from *Eight Minutes from the Sun*, ©1983, are reprinted by permission of Saturday Press, Upper Montclair, NJ, and selections from *Family Life*, ©1988, are reprinted by permission of Story Line Press, Brownsville, OR.

The new poems in this collection originally appeared, some in slightly different form, in these publications whose editors I would like to thank:
Poetry Miscellany, "Belgian Flicks"; *Three Rivers Poetry Journal*, "Getting Under Way," "Guarding the Unrevealed"; *Northwest Review*, "The Entry of James Ensor into My Memories of Brussels"; *Chowder Review*, "Bayscenes, Childhood"; *West Branch*, "Foster Mother Dee's Departure," "Mirror," "The Recluse," "Ruby Scenes of Autumn Losses"; *Laurel Review*, "Taking Calls in Freeport, New York"; *North American Review*, "The Bequest"; *Michigan Quarterly Review*, "River House Inventions"; *American Voice*, "Santa Cruz Idyll"; *Raccoon*, "Seine-et-Oise"; *13th Moon*, "Conspicuous Ability in Literature"; *Colorado Quarterly*, "The Children Are Going to Far Places"; *Amelia*, "Max Is Asked to Reach into the Past for Memories"; *Exquisite Corpse*, "Maybe"; *Ploughshares*, "Midwest Albas"; "Daughter's Photo in an Old Folks Home"; *Crosscurrents*, "Riverwalk"; *Columbia Magazine*, "Shaking the Man Awake"; *Helicon Nine*, "Glenn"; *Memphis State Review*, "The Leavetaking," "Advice to a Writer Imagining Conception and Birth"; *Denver Quarterly*, "Seeing Music in Winter"; *Belle Lettres*, "Off Route 303 in the County"; *Poetry Northwest*, "Early June Meditation at Lakeside," "Men and Women of the Xingu Forest," "Ohio Letters"; *California Quarterly*, "The Mad Shepherd"; *New Virginia Review*, "The Boy in the Pool"; *Missouri Review*, "Lines for Eastern Bluebirds"; *Chelsea Review*, "Animal Bodies in Virginia"; *New Letters*, "Lost Letters"; *The Cream City Review*, "The Dance of Adolph and Eva"; *Caliban*, "The Trapper and the Arctic Fox."

"What Are the Days" from *Family Life* won a 1986 Pushcart Prize; "The Letters of a Name" from *Eight Minutes from the Sun* appeared in *The Yearbook of American Poetry Anthology of Magazine Verse*, Monitor Books & Company. *The Woman Who Loved Worms* won the Great Lakes Colleges Association National First Book Award. *Family Life* was a finalist for The Poet's Prize.

GETTING UNDER WAY:
NEW AND SELECTED POEMS

For S. A. S.

Table of Contents

EIGHT MINUTES FROM THE SUN

FAMILY LIFE

NEW POEMS

THE WOMAN WHO LOVED WORMS

ORPHANS OF ALL DENOMINATIONS WILL MEET

(from a sign in the 96th Street subway)

Orphans of all denominations will meet
in Tierra del Fuego orphanage grounds
near the sign that says:
> Do Not Step on the Orphans
>
> Do Not Smoke the Orphans

they've been burned enough
in the sizzling lake that shines like the smile
of Razzle Bath the sleuth man.

Orphans of all denominations will meet in Heidelberg
near the autobahn sign that says:
> Achtung!
>
> Do Not Pick the Orphans

from out of the grass where they memorize lice on the pillows.

Budhist, Shinto, Bahai, Seventh Day, Animist orphans
will meet in Mali near the airport sign that says:
> Check All Orphans
>
> With the Baggageman

and buckle them in to dream of passage like doomed geese
stunned with corn and gorged for the feast of organs.

Orphans of all remunerations, 50-cent orphans, living wage
orphans, minus-the-price-of-abortion orphans will meet
in Valdosta near the sign that says:
> Put an Orphan in Your Tank

and see the longer miles he smiles in the speed of forgetting
orphanage picnics the empire packs in throwaway time.

Be nice to the orphans. They want to suffer shipshape lives
in our ribald state which is dying in all denominations
near the sign that says:
                    No Disrobing Orphans on the Beach
offenses will be met on orphanage grounds—
disposable minds and redeemable whips
free to the keeper of orphans.

A COLLAR ROUNDS MY THOUGHTS

Priest, my father, priest,
your collar cuts my neck,
my resonating breath's
intake
at knowing you were naked,
the collar jettisoned,
a crescent on the floor
where the bed upheld
my mother's pity for your sex.
Your strict lips kissed
her thirty years of fear,
kissed them away,
her dainty bones
under your own
barely moving
like the quarter moon
lighting the room,
like the tightening collar
caught in the light
choking desire
in the penitent hours
before my birth.
Priest, my father, priest,
your collar rounds my thought
like a moon, refractory and white.

Latin scholar, library dust
on your face, glossing tomes
next to her breath.
Only intellect

before her flesh
set your loins on edge.
Then transfixed
desiring her
as the lame desire miracles.
Two scholars at dusk.
Not Heloise nor Abelard,
neither their youth
nor calamitous love.
Priest, my father, priest,
your collar rounds my world
like an equator
burning to know your life
interred forever in that faith
which primed your guilt.
No stigma on the grave,
only your name witnessed by rain
and I, your bastard child.

REMEMBERING THE DANCES

She died of cirrhosis and was laid out
on a marble lounge, pickled-beet dark lips
tasting taffeta and salt.

He went on unplugged, dragging his cord
like a telephone, out-of-order, vandalized,
remembering the dances: Lambeth Walk, the Shag, the Truck.

Nevermind the gin-blurred drives
to any dive the turnpike flashed.

Remembering the dances.
Five fundamental steps to quickened bliss
on the Arthur Murray Plan.

Turkey Trot and Lindy Hop
blotting up the raw egg light of morning.

Remembering the dances smooth as frozen daiquiris,
dipping straws in the world's chilled glass.

Nevermind the crumpling legs after the dances,
flesh too etherized to speak.
Money's rumba swung their hips
swizzling the Conga, Mambo, Argentine Tango.

Dancing to remember the dances.
Dancing to remember not dancing
was formaldehyde, syringe bags of blood.
No Irene Castle in the afterworld of shut down bars.

"One more drinkee" for the floating road
that reeled inside the ward. Tapping stars
in the ballroom sky, Cugat's throb and plush, big bands
remembering

she was his party favor,
freshly pleated and hoorayed,
whiskeys away, martini standard time
in the foxtrot lounge of yesterdays.

Packing his attachments like a vacuum cleaner man,
he sells the goods to anyone, even himself
in the closing hours after her death
and takes a belt of rye to sweep aside
all the steps they took in between the dances.

MOVIE MANAGER, PARIS, FRANCE

L'Odéon, black cookie box
dotted with crumbs.
I'm propped inside
near a movie sky
that sings in French.

Suddenly, the volume's off.
Dialogue of sickness,
myself and my legs.
The lurching aisle
spills me into soundlessness.

Awake from collapse;
the movie manager's
rubbery hand
under my blouse.

Ah, merde. A jet of spit
from my pretzel mouth.
Saliva in his squat moustache.

His steaming eyes
like two fresh drops
of country dung,
enriching my pity,
fattening my rage.

Good news! Nilda is back
the sign huzzahs
in the Beauty Shoppe

as the rain combs
the sky over and over
like a grandmother combing
the hair of a child.

Impermanent waves
of rain on the street;
the trees are straight
but the city bends.

Nilda is back
from Guayaquil,
Quito, Ponce, San Jose

to tease the gringo smiles
of blue-eyed wives
in the raining city.

And now she cha chas up the aisles
to supervise the upswept lines
of an aging lady

who does not know why Nilda comes
or why she goes
or where her hair uncurls at night
damp at the edge from waves of love.

DR. INEZ

I'm a resident, Dr. Inez, touring the wards.
These rooms I walk contain superb
examples of degenerate sorrow.
My instructors outline stages of decay
which they in turn excise,
bearing their trays of implements.
Blueplate cures and bogus hopes. Curettage.
Curés of cures.

The cold wind scrapes my eyes,
onward go the spectacles; cafeteria selections,
dishy, broad delectables, eggplant breasts, but
malignant eyes like tumors
spreading lies about my skill.

A chill. Autumn's critical condition.
Must I scrutinize the blood, urine, gangrene
in the leaves?
I, Dr. Inez, sincere, not yet coarsened by events,
circumnavigating pain, the hapless Lourdes of suffering,
amputee processionals to a light
some quack child dreams
fattening her father's coin at the bank.

Tomorrow's snow winds bandages.
I will confess to patched-up truths;
the press of wretchedness,
leprous fingers at my throat,
and must devise a better way
to stick like tape in a dampening room
before time's blade prepares to cut
the central valve to all I love.

MEETING IN LONDON

That I leapt from her hips, her tidy legs soiled
with my cries into forceps; the looming nurse and intern,
masked bandits, rifling my mother's womb like a bank.

And from the steel-precision hospital, a Wermacht band,
I smartly marched, oompah...pah, Zieg Heil,
into Third Reichs of my childhood. Ya!

Now drab, brown hours in the silence, the sun,
a faucet dripping time, my mother a forest, winterwood:
birch and ravelling oak,
damp waves pinched along the neck,

her glances drifting on my lips, my face
reflecting dread, (she'd abandoned me, like Munich,
and trusted the regime).

I call her name across the rubble.
Achtung! You will love me,
the thought clicked heels,
though my Nazis float in a limbo of Jews
who turned in their own children.

Auf wiedersehen. One gold molar in her mouth,
the only gaudiness, device to memorize her smile
in the squeezed-out light, lemony and dry,
the sky over London in a bowler hat, palest grey, invisible.

MURDERING NUMBERS

Soissy-sur-École, unstintingly French,
have been there with a plow
tilling numbers and non-numbers
in the school rain, smudged arithmetic,
problems in chalk; dowdy captive to a desk,
and chained to mademoiselle's voice,
the gusseted serge of her proper dress.

Rain-glyphs on the windowpane;
I tried to break the code, assured that the script
opened locks to a drenched world
of storm kings, cloud queens, thunderous bosoms
that lightning bid the populace
to cower in their huts
until a prince was found for the princess:
rain-droplet eyes, white tulip breasts,

but was ferruled into fractions,
mutilated digits, numbers on the chopping-block,
dissected in half and less than whole,
the unwholesome practice of minus signs,
these wounded ciphers less than
those decapitated ones. A hospital of numbers,
slashed, crippled, hobbling on the blackboard.

The land outside the room
luminously plus in the lavender light.
It was where I wanted to count froth, grass,
inconsequentially dazzling leaves reading the rain,

inimical to grocery lists, recipes halved,
bank interest and loans, things math was good for
in the gray-serge freshly ironed town where I was from,

but stayed after school, rain-script erased,
memories of rain stored in the chalk.
In the chalk-dust room I slaughtered fractions,
my diagonal knife's stab-stab,
absurd reductions into air,
the globe I wrote on like the zero I would get
in Soissy-sur-École when I was there
murdering numbers.

EMPRESS IN THE MIRROR

With high-jewelled hair
the empress in the mirror
dallies:

jars of wax, powder, cotton,
kohl and rouge,
chessmen in a game of beauty.

Floating her pen on linen paper,
ink flying into wings of script,

that empress mocks my workday bones
which close me as a shutter
darkens the room of an invalid girl,

and sips my light while I scrape stones
for priestly secrets,
my eyes in their hoods like drunken monks

dreaming wine, monastic love,
arcane parchments where abbeys moved
their cauldrons for a fiendish lord.

My knees more ridged than a drudge's face,
her eloquent legs.

Imprisoned in my mirror, that empress says:
"I am to you as onyx is to gravel,"
pelting words to small enclosures
of my skull.

AMAZON

A grip of orchids in the forest jaws,
and moaning lianas
caught in the morning fog of gauze
and the waking river.

Tribesmen sang to the cayman river, to the toucan river.
It was their mother straddling the moon, riding the water.
Amazon.

Tribal songs now clot in the throat,
silenced by embezzlers, and the *fazandeiro*
from his throne of guns. Blasted kingdoms
where Xingus thrived knowing no word for "punishment."

Corte de baneiro, backward and forward swing of the blade,
slice of two heads in a single thrust,
and *corte maior* cleaving the tribesman
into two or more parts to thud on the ground—
blood jerking like a palsied snake to the river's pit.
Warrior river. Mourner of tribesmen.

Great sister-bird, the Cessna, vomiting bombs
while in the forest a girl hangs down, legs tied apart
as a rubber tapper chops her in half.

Huitoto, Crao, Ticuna men,
the river turns its cobbled skin
like a white city in the moon.
Green-plumed river, cayman of water,
mirror to the sun's blazing ribs of light.

At night, the land's mouth, emerald thirst,
spiked teeth and tongue in the marmoset's scream
taking the river into its dream,
exhaling water. Amazon.

THE WOMAN WHO LOVED WORMS

(from a Japanese legend)

Disdaining butterflies
as frivolous,
she puttered with caterpillars,
and wore a coarse kimono,
crinkled and loose at the neck.

Refused to tweeze her brows
to crescents,
and scowled beneath dark bands
of caterpillar fur.

Even the stationery
on which she scrawled
unkempt calligraphy,
startled the jade-inlaid
indolent ladies,
whom she despised
like the butterflies
wafting kimono sleeves
through senseless poems
about moonsets and peonies;
popular rot of the times.

No, she loved worms,
blackening the moon of her nails
with mud and slugs,
root gnawing grubs,
and the wing case of beetles.

And crouched in the garden,
tugging at her unpinned hair,
weevils queuing across her bare
and unbound feet.

Swift as wasps, the years.
Midge, tick and maggot words
crowded her haikus
and lines on her skin turned her old,
thin as a spinster cricket.

Noon in the snow pavilion,
gulping heated sake
she recalled Lord Unamuro,
preposterous toad
squatting by the teatray,
proposing with conditions
a suitable marriage.

Ha! She stoned imaginary butterflies,
and pinching dirt,
crawled to death's cocoon
dragging a moth to inspect
in the long afternoon.

GREENLAWN DAYS

(for my foster grandmother)

She took me Saturdays on the Beeline bus,
past hick towns belching after lunch,
to the cemetery gate. Greenlawn days.

And said, "I always hated waste,"
clenching my arm like a prize,
her free hand nabbing rose bouquets,
miniature flags and picture frames,
a rheumy focus in her eyes
under the sky's farsightedness.

Sizing her plot, a scraggy mound,
viewed by mausoleums,
their popeyed angels hoisting scrolls,

she made me read the names, the proper dead,
blunted under sediment,
lulled by verses in the turning star
I hated for its slowness in making me grow.

Old woman, old woman, my shield and my wound,
I saw her grow frail in the stone of each sun,
hammered down to eighty years of blindness,
unreformed when the casket closed
and lowered to a stingy grave;

crabgrass and wasps squandering their poems
common rhymes for a scavenger lady
I wanted to love.

ALIVE AND TAKING NAMES

0-5   Centers of ossification appear as I squall
"wyde in this world wonderes to hear."
The light my second amnion.
Mother like a frog, white exhausted thighs
precede my deciduous teeth, the better to bite
the asylum where I didn't earn my keep.
Ward of the state and stable criteria.

5-12   Acetabular elements join.
Ilium, ischium, pubis,
a little hen's breast against my hands.
In the corpulent dark, hearing children grow
a song of bones as the moon climbed
and ovary bells, my eggs and the moon
tolling each month.

12-15   Epiphysial union of long bones.
Long bones in my stride,
glib nights, counterfeit smiles,
trumped-up charges against what I loved.
Years blindly eating childhood's fat.
Knowledge like a shield
wounds when pressed too near.

25-36   Active vault suture closing.
Active designs in the skull.
Delicate zippers sealing in
the stars, interstellar dust,
brackets of marriage, and one short birth
shaped like a comma between two worlds.

36-50   Lipping of scapular glenoid fossa.
       Fossa, a ditch.
       I have not come to it.
       Fossa, an abyss.
       I wait for the master archeologist
       to dig and pick,
       tweezers plucking artifacts,
       my trail of refuse and souvenirs.

50 plus   Quasi pathological erosions of bone.
       The pendulum's pit.
       My old electrons blow their fuse.
       Dark pond.
       My mother like a frog,
       white exhausted thighs collapsed.

plus   What did it mean to play
       a xylophone of bones?
       An octave of stone. Delight. Decrease,
       bleached lips dim against my fingers
       closing in a stiffening fist,
       dumb warrior
       pitted against eloquent death,
       illiterate mulch for those whose squalls
       will go "wyde in this world
       wonderes to hear,"
       the light their second amnion.

HOME MOVIE OF POLAND

for Saul

A picnic table. The family assembles.
As if in a dream you are small,
your cousin squints, his shredded hair
later deloused at Bergen-Belsen.
Grandfather swatting flies. It is summer,
gentile, undulating blond.
Grandma sews a button on.

Nearby, the house stoked with bread
warm as the bed
you and mama slept in
like a closed parenthesis
in Poland's sad, long sentence.

Elsewhere, the Fuhrer's bloody moon
rising in Sudetenland, plans for decimation.

They were so old, Noah and Sarah,
old and thin as rain,
easy to close the valve of their lives
as he bent to the news like a birch in the wind.
Grandma seizing her only hen
for a future of eggs. Auschwitz freight.
Jerusalem, if I forget thee,
let me lose my right arm.
God has plucked you out of the disease.
The frames fade, white phlox and blood
shedding their scent in a closet of dreams.

Rescued.
That your mother and father
hunched in a room to make you come true
like a glistening egg,
that will not crack
for any Wehrmacht omelette.

Your hair fringed like Polish stars
in a telescope of nights
when the moon was removed to Bergen-Belsen
in the final solution of moons.

Do not forget Jerusalem,
my love in a western land,
America, America where we live in a film
spooling forward and back in the speed of events
unreal as the light
that blinks in our eyes after hours of darkness.

LISTENING TO DVORAK'S SERENADE IN E

Everything has ripened,
the oranges glisten
in their sharp worlds,
the apples have broken
their juice
in my mouth.
I am alone at the edge
of all the gold seasons,
a tide of clouds
bearing me home
like a migratory bird.

And this bright music
shaping dancers
on a bitter dust of roads,
divining rods
that point
to a further distance:
stone, water, stone.

Dowser, find my deep stream.
Builder, make my house
to last in the ochre heart
of the falling sun,
in this shining harvest.

Monks of the Years for Zodiacal Ears

Actuary, Fritillary, Mush
Mandrill, Mace, Jejune,
Jelly, Aghast, Septic Ember,
Oak Toner, Remember, Distemper

Device to Mesmerize the Monks

30 days hath septic ember
mandrill jejeune and remember
all the rest have 31 dyes
of different color:

Actuary: puce   Mush: buff
Mace: rose   Jelly: lime
Aghast: jade   Oak Toner: rust
Distemper: slush

except Fritillary which howls
28 cold tones of dust.

APOTHEGMS AND COUNSELS

If someone says you're too short,
say diamond pins don't come in cartons.

If someone says you're too large,
say you're an Amazon at large.

If someone says your breasts are too big,
say you bought them in Katmandu
and the fitting rooms were dark.

Say chickpeas are loved in Prague
if someone says your breasts are too small.

How much do you weigh on the sun? On the moon?

Tons on the sun.
Less on the moon.
Love makes you weightless.

If someone says you're too far out,
say Doppler Effect,
that you're writing a history of light
for the children of Pythagoras.

SPANISH HEAVEN

My heaven is Hispanic ladies in satin tube dresses,
their hair like a chocolate sundae melts into waves.
They are giving me transparent nightgowns
and kisses on my face.
Lotteria tickets bulging in my purse.
They are saying *que bonita* in the house
of their throats
and we all eat mangoes and fritos d'amor
selling Avon products to each other forever.

And damning Fidel, Trujillo, what bums.
But Evita, what heart and Elizabeth Taylor
there in her shrine,
Monacos of pleasure as Grace took our hand.
Eyepads of freedom, Avons of love.

Mascara of angels, hairspray of God,
they are teasing my hair like a heavenly cloud
while the acid of husbands eating alone
rumbles Dolores, *putas* and rape
in the hell of machismo.

DEANNA DURBIN, COME HOME

(Deanna Durbin was born in Canada and now resides in France)

We melted; liquid cherry centers,
vanilla-colored lozenges
in balconies,
emporiums of movie dust,
committed the dark to memory

as Deanna beamed, Funiculi, Funicula
in her strapless gown
fluttering High C
to our hicktown's popcorn litter.
It was a better world of bluebirds,
usherette bliss, rectangular light
as the screen snapped on
the umptyum years.

Deanna Durbin. The columns say
she parles with the crème de la crème
in France. Entre nous, quel ennui!
I wish she'd come home. The Mounties hunt
her trebled notes out near Lake Louise.
Time takes a breakneck tour of whatever happened
to whom and where. Despotic love of memories.

Deanna Durbin. I want her baby orchid throat
singing GOIN' HOME, the way it used to be
when the light poured in like a blizzard
and I floated home humming the theme,
unblinking faith in moviehouse shrines,
transparent ends, wholehearted gods,
     Funiculi, Funicula.

ALIVE AND TAKING NAMES

If I set out to list ointments
would I find myself slick,
ceaselessly involved
in salves, balms, daubs, smears,
referencing spikenard, lotion, pomade,
greasing the wheels, as it were, of my skin?

Best to forego fat, the oleaginous stuff
that lards the heart.

If I set out to list ills, ague, pox, bloody flux,
would I find myself sick,
ceaselessly involved in croup, rot,
referencing bran, drugging the fool
in the ward of my skull?

Best to forego pain, the surgical brain
doesn't love nouns.

Croaker, monger, medic, quack,
sawbones, prober, jawsmith, vet,
I am well, sound, hale, cross referenced with fit,
snuffling the morning air, alive and taking names.

CHATEAUNEUF DU PAPE, THE POPE'S VALET SPEAKS

Your miter must sit well
as the Duchess of Windsor sits well
on her horse,

correctness counts, the crozier gleams,
your chasubles are freshly pressed.

This day reminds me of Moët et Chandon,
little bubbles in a Vatican air,
the sun to kneel in burgundies.
Non vintage champaign for the Bishop of Lièges,
that Flemish hulk of gutturals.

As you say, we need our zealots, dear Nuncio.
Stay with your bulls. Do not eschew
miraculous fish, the savor of loaves.

This wine is new-fangled,
an impetuous nun. I must confess
to disheveled dreams.

Infallibility calls for meat, steak tartare,
skewered lambs in a shiskabob
from the Levantine.

I once had a prioress in Tripoli kissing
the tongue of my shoe. This wine absolves me
of my infamy. Ah, love that miserere
for two voices.

The room spins its Vatican roulette.
La la la. What wine is this? A bottle
of golden syllables. Yes, your flock clamors
for directions:

norths of venison, Kyrie Eleison, easts of veal,
souths of pork, wests of tripe, papem in aspic,
harum, scarum, cake angelorum,
omnia vincit Armour baloney.

What's that pounding at our door?

The Bishop of Lièges
asks your holiness to bless
the bilingual gluttons of Belgium.

OLD WOMAN, ESKIMO

Her singing makes
the rain fall.
Her sewing brings clouds.
When she stops sewing,
the green weather comes.
When she stops singing,
the white weather comes
full of smooth threads
to sew up her song.

She has seen birth,
children waiting
for their names.

When she stops seeing,
the snow needles come
sewing the land
to the hem of the sky.
In her dream she is
a bone needle
that will not thread.
The hides come undone
all her songs are gone
inside the rain
for her children
to hear later on.

QUESTIONS FOR DISCUSSION

1.
To what extent do you love?
To a large extent in a line
of plovers going south.

How do you justify kisses
coming like plovers from Baffin Bay,
back and forth
between narration and tears?

The omissions that seem most important
aren't here to judge.
Love hovered in the courtroom,
a hummingbird drawn to a perfumed vial.

2.
In what sense of the word did you sing?
Shboom. The setting was significant.
Twenty years of birds
flying south to Uruguay.

How did you isolate the gold dust factor
from problems of flight in a given range?
His flight, my range, home on the sofa
with an antelope's ounce of intention to stay
as opposed to buffaloes, as opposed to clouds.

On what grounds did you sight the terns?
In the pearl-gray mantle of the fog.
In our ornithology, he was my finch,
I, his crow. He was my cardinal, I, his nun
flying towards a perfect vow. Christ, I do.

We will meet from time to time
in a garden of Dominicans.
Adios, Brother Gold.
Our vanishing act won't wash
the glittering questions away.

NOVEMBER LORD

I have gathered the melons,
my skull is a gourd,
earth, my pumpkin
rolls each night
a hallow's eve
of mindless craft.

A raucous autumn
rattling its stick
on the drum of my skull.
Tight-skinned hours
passive to the sadist baton of the sun.

Ego and grandeur conduct their tones.
I am pitched to love like a crow
ravening the gold harvest.
My sleek coat glistens, bituminous coal
in a mineshaft of shadows.

Where will the find go? Gold in a sieve,
fugitive rock all turning dark,
rituals in a field untended
by the Inca prince, the stunning Atahualpa
in his harvest of death.

Time will comb the gold debris.
Our mouths in the amber of an eon's kiss.
But philologer, my prince sends word,
I cross the bridge into kingdoms of light.
Viracocha, November Lord,
the melons are gathered beneath a gaunt moon
which spins like my heart.

NICOLETTE

Nicolette, my little carrot,
I pull you out of the dark ground
of Pennsylvania
where they blasted my thighs
and scraped your seed away.

You are twelve, my counterpart child
breathlessly running into rooms
with acorns and leaves
you want to arrange
for the most senseless beauty.

I have married your father.
We are reconciled to minus signs.

The moist kiss you give me
comes from the forest
of a dark time;

anthracite in the earth,
old signals from the stars
when I walked away from the kill,
blood on my legs, a phrase to caulk
the falling walls in a universe
moving light years away
from our promises.

Nicolette, we will meet
in my poem and when the light
calls your name
you will rise like a fern
to live all summer long,
a green integer
in a pure equation of song.

A crystal teardrop
from the collection
of Madame des Larmes.
I want Dresden.
My voice's alarm
at the front of its box.
The finest Sèvres.
Gold-rimmed everything.

That I was queen of the orphans
when we lived in a burlap sack
everyone knows.
I won't let them forget
the welts I caught
in those corridors.

Service for two,
I shall dine with myself.
Duchess of pity
demitasse cups;
mother-of-pearl on the knives
that I may cut
my mother in half
like a Florida prawn.

This and that Limoges.
I like the word tureen.
What owls say to rats

in Ireland.
It's not enough.
It's not enough.
The fruitwood doesn't match
my dream.

I shall dine with my past,
that chattering child
plain as a pan
spattering news of peregrine birds.

Take her away.
Put her in a muffin tin
into the pantry and out of my time.
Her parents didn't keep her.
Monsignor La La and Lady Correct
went off to sup on miracles.

Truth Lady, what do you see
in my palm?
Strength of character
and a curious fate
of sidestepping wreckage
in a perishing state.
Nothing gold-rimmed.

EIGHT MINUTES FROM THE SUN

ALL THINGS ARE ONE, SAID EMPODOCLES
IN A LIGHT AS PROBABLE AS HUME

Immanuel Kant sets his clock
in another warp of Germany? Could be.
In any event, the sun's slow watch
ticks off a time for the snowgeese to fly
from our sentences and paragraphs.

Fine words won't butter the parsnips, you quip.
Agreed. Tonight the stars will strike
unreasonable facts in the dark
of Sagittarius as I look for an arrow
of light and tell you the story of Orion

bringing the spoils of the chase to Merope,
his legendary love. You accuse me of loving
bookwords, "eleemosynary," "asseverate"
when you open your wine of a good recent year.

Dizzy and skimping over syllables, later
we see The Hunter with his sword pointing
to our door from his forest in the galaxy.

So many times I have heard our murmuring
at the top of the stairs, the habits of speech
we let go as we climb towards the night's disorders
and dreams, for this is the way we lock out the dark

in its autumn constellation, above precise assemblages
of trees, their orderly sorrow of changing leaves,
in the middle of a continent, paw paw, basswood,
hawthorn, ash.

THE LETTERS OF A NAME

How many names for what the bees see?
Leaves hear them humming in the blueprint
of eons to come in the summer.

How many names for what the leaves see?
Figure an angle of the sun's descent.
Go draw a flower to the light.
Marigolds, Four O'Clocks.

Some are made to tally up sums
of artifacts, spoor, fossil remains,
to count the letters of a name.
Not I with my back to the St. John's Fire

in a garden where you sketch me
in a few, brief strokes
starting with the circle of my eyes.
How many names for what they see in waves

of the evening? Blue rising in the stem
of a flame, the fastening on of stars
to the sky, is not listed in the manual
of how love looks in a crouched position.

Tomorrow you will draw me out of the shadows.
Tomorrow I will let you take my name away.

HOLDING ON

I hear the short and wiry rains
switching on and off like a jittery fuse,
lost stations on a fading band,
episodes of our narrative.

Repairing small breaks in the flow
of words, you go on transmitting
messages I decode by fits and starts.

We are holding on, my sometimes like-minded
love, even while I watch a one-legged bird
on a lawn whose worms are running out of luck.

Fitful rain. I pour my days through a sieve,
try to milk the ram, open the stable door,
but the frazzled horse is gone
along with the sun.

I want a break in the clouds, to catch
a scrap of song for good, but things to mend,
hammer in, screw, tape, caulk go on multiplying

like the mosquitoes we swatted the other day
when we decided once more to back the right horse,
go further and fare well,
to mark out a course on the way.

1
Dazed, a birch leaf sails downstream
out of the hubbub of hornets and bees
raiding the field.
Here, where the river slows its course,
I watch the print of a snail's back
repeat in spirals of water.

2
In slow motion, my body turns
through a keyhole of light
out of the forest and into the meadow.
Springtails and mites
seem to study slantwise light on moss
like geometers.
In a margin of grass, a cricket stops
to revise its ancient argument.

3
Its back scored with six black notes
on an orange field, the beetle clings
in a curled up nest of Queen Anne's lace.
Rippling hours in waves, the day
embraces dragonflies and wasps, a katydid
skipping a beat on its narrow scale,
a finch's wing skimming the thistle.

4

From distant cornrows, a lone crow calls.
Drugged on goldenrod and vervain, the field
lies open mouthed in a dream.
Drowsy, I stumble on the river's branch,
a languorous stream, but when I turn
my back, the sassafras tree jolts into gold,
the red oak, brown.

5

What is to come sleeps in the bud
now tilting upwards towards a thinning light.
Later, as I trace the path, the river passes
out of sight.

FOREST CHILDREN

We heard swifts feeding in air,
sparrows ruffling dusty feathers,
a tapping on stones, mud, snow, pulp
when rain came down, the hiss of fire.
Counting bird eggs in a dome of twigs,
we heard trees fall and learned
to name them on a page for school.

And living among trees, in the shadows
of their leaves and seeds, we had
the mystery of numbers, we believed,
from figuring angles of the sun
or counting stumps in a widening field.
Each day saws subtracted boughs
for books of double algebra, equations
in a text we carried home
past hacked down pines.

Conjuring the spirit of the grove,
in a circle we sang:
"mark out planes of shade and light
that seedlings might root."
One morning in spring
trees showed winter skeletons
through smoke, abrupt curves, bent oak.
We were stripped of words to cast a spell.

"Algebra cadabra," someone shouted
pointing to a vanished nest
we remembered as braided of moss,
ivy tendrils and spider's silk.

MAYFLIES

The god of mayflies allots his creatures years
in a watery larval world, but fixes their dance
in air to a span of hours or days. There are
windrows of their corpses, soft, rotting piles under
street lights or scattered imperceptibly in the small
debris of pond edges and beaches in spring at day's
end. After leaving circles of weeds and fish, nymphs
which fed on pond scum and the grit of leaves, bloom
into soft-bodied flies with short feelers smooth
as blades of hair. The many-veined wings are
transparent as an onion peel or a tiny swatch of silk,
and when idle ride the glistening body like a sail.
Long and supple for clasping the mate over water
at night, male forelegs do their probing work. Nocturnal,
mayflies fast for the nuptial flight, and sometimes
before they drop from the rigors of desire and age,
appear in swarms like a finely stippled cloud
of furious life.

SPRING LUNCH

for Sophie

The goat cheese glows like a snow
so pure the King of Ch'in
and Emperor Wu would have ordered it
to court. Your hair, too, is the color
of the moon in the middle of the day.
No Book of Change can describe the steady
eloquence of your ways in this and that art.

"Within the earth, a mountain,"
the I-Ching says. We speak of climbing
in a dream, of the equipoise between two
contrasting elements. My pleasure
is a mountain.

The five-pointed star of the sweetgum
leaf and the fan-shaped ginkgo share
in the contours of spring. We eat almond
cakes, I, swallowing greedily, you with
dainty hands, like a court lady who chants
the poems of Li-Shang-yin.

Sipping wine, I hesitate to leave.
A hundred times when I was a child
I said thank you to my guardians and
didn't mean a word. Now I am grateful
for the gift of our constancy
over years of change.

When, at last, I leave, I turn my face
to you in a light-hearted kiss, and
set out for the city under a sky
blossoming clouds.

TRIPTYCH

Neither moved by suffering
nor joy in good works, a woman
gathers anise for the evening
rice. She would fly looking back
like the ibis but stays in her place
where nothing wills the stones to move.

Elsewhere, a potter dizzy with the memory
of spinning clay stays in his place
painting tall mullein, gray-green velvet
leaves and yellow flowers luring
orioles and swallowtails.

The world is dizzy with the memory
of spinning days, the poet writes
stirring sage tea in still another place,
ignorant of the woman whose musings
only now begin to take shape like a young
river. No one sees her when she falls

from a precipice, not the ibis
looking back as it flies, nor the potter
dreaming of porcelain formulas, not even
the poet who invents a gathering of anise
at day's end. Still the western mountains
rise to meet a chronicle of light
read from the farthest sky.

STARTALK IN THE GREEK LUNCHEONETTE

A boy is talking about infinity.
I hope he's right. I hate closed
worlds, big bangs, and keep a light
on in the dark. From where I sit
the galaxies ought to keep
running their blurs to the rim
and out beyond that, scuffling up
stars for the boy to take in
as he talks.

The boy? He looks about ten
with a good head for math.
"You ought to own a pair of skates,"
somebody says in the booth.
Roller derby champs
haven't read Isaac Newton
or Tycho Brahe. Does it matter?
A boy is talking about the universe.
Right? Trillions of miles, he says.

IN IRELAND

along the shore
those are the strivers
after high romance, a blade
of seagrass in her blouse,
saltmarks on his boots.

They have sent out
a tangle of half-meant words
to the wind which cries
like a conch blown from
the hill.

Arms entwined, they shamble by.
Neither sees the priest
ready to pounce with scripture
and verse. He would beat
their longings with a cross.

Neither looks up at the clouds
nor out to the sea
which strums the bones of couples
and priests in a delicate air
the fish hear through waves.

ALONG THE GARONNE

There has always been a road
for wandering daughters, past signs
in another tongue, unfamiliar doors,
vestibules and halls.

In my mother's room ghosts sighed:
"Who are you to make claims?"
"Lovechild," I answer in a river town
of cypress and palm,
floodmarks on the house
from an old spring torrent.

My mother and father. Once they walked
through a stream of fragrances, nodded
and stopped, watched hummingbirds shift from bloom
to bloom. Here where I've come to wrangle
with wills and lump sums, he read a passage
from Linnaeus' *Species Plantarum*,
she fiddled with her gloves.

Beyond bequest and deed, they seem
players in a dream fixed fast to the stage,
and held by light like carvings
on my mother's comb which arranged
her rippling hair when she was a girl
and the clouds above the river climbed
one over the other as they do before rain.

In a rain that leaves a road to children
off to school, birds find shelter
where they will. I wait for their song,
and along the Garonne put down these words to say
birds sang when I was born, and will fly known paths
above the cloud of my mother's hair,
my father's books, fading and closed
west of the river's meandering streams.

NOTES FROM A GUTTED HOUSE

Waiting to remember theorems,
isthmuses, and litmus tests
I dozed through school
and dawdled home
where the parent wars went on
in an arsenal of booze.

Besotted sergeants
dreaming cadences
I couldn't hear, they woke
geared to fight.
Day after day, I wanted to find
them charred, orders half-
singed at the back
of their throats.

Now a plume of smoke writes its last
command from the gutted house.
The combatants are released. Fall's
sequences repeat a downward drift
of intervals and leaves, hickory, gold,
garnet in the tupelo. The same red
chevron in the oak is a tanager or
a cardinal phrasing its song

as my burnt-out masters cool
their heels underground.
And waiting for parallel lines

to meet, for brackets to vanish
in algebra, I crane my neck
to sight-read the birds, the small notes
of their flight streaming like music.

A FAITHFUL LIKENESS

Saint Francis, press this day into your book
of praise, and I'll vow to learn the music
of Aquila, galactic bird in the migrating
dark, right after I catch a faithful likeness
of the immature blue goose, uniformly dusky
with dusky feet. Do I turn here?

At last, a blur of fire: red-winged
blackbirds in a grove. The music? Slurred
notes that disappear like arrowheads in
a small avalanche of leaves. I want to draw
the red wing's epaulets, the vireo's red eye,
its white eyebrow bordered in black.

Yesterday, I read "emblems of perfection"
in a daybook, a monk's phrase for birds
in flight. Today, a string of geese flies
overhead like a circumflex leaning on its side.
Do I turn there?

Mother of trails, give me the wit to find
my way while I can see the gray jay's white
forehead and throat. Before night sets in
I want to chance upon its eggs in a bowl
of twigs and bark, Saint Francis, to define
these nests and marks before I leave
the woods, to do so with ease.

LAKE SONG

Every day our name is changed,
say stones colliding into waves.
Go read our names on the shore,
say waves colliding into stones.

Birds over water call their names
to each other again and again
to say where they are.
Where have you been, my small bird?

I know our names will change one day
to stones in a field
of anemones and lavender.

Before you read the farthest wave,
before our shadows disappear
in a starry blur, call out your name
to say where we are.

FAMILY LIFE

GASCON JOURNEY

I have set out to meet her
for the last time, to examine
a face that resembles mine
in one corner above the right eye
and in a temple vein.
Fontainebleu, Tours, Poitiers,
Angoulême. The train feeds
the voyager a dream of calm.
My mother and father, their secrets
hummed like rails, flew through
road beds and coupling cars.
Unlikely lovers.
"I'd almost forgotten," she will sigh.
"Why do you persist?" She won't look
into my eyes. I'll watch her turn away
after I leave. A flutter of a memory
too swift to catch will vanish in a meadow,
a corridor of trees. Was it her face
bent over my crib? Were her shoulders
hunched when she whispered to the priest?
What did she confess to him?
I almost see her, my rare and somber visitor,
the mother nuns said was a cousin or an aunt.
The long aisle of lies. I also sigh. I,
unknown to the few of a thinning clan,
have come this far to see a blood stranger.
Bordeaux, Agen, Nérac, Espiens.
There are questions I will never ask.
There are answers she will never give.

EVENT HORIZONS

1

A flame crests in the fireplace.
Loose ashes and flurries of snow scatter
in a California winter.
The caped figure, hurried up the stairs,
is the midwife who eases my father
into dawn. Heavy velvet drapes are drawn.
Grandfather twirls a brandy glass and
lifts it to the light. A son to carry
his likeness and his name, their names
emblazoned in gold letters on a door.
He draws on a cigar, watches a cloud
of smoke rise and disperse. A tiny bubble sits
on the baby's lips, then breaks. Sleep.
Soon to receive his first dream, the boy
is ignorant of boundaries and time. He
has not learned the meaning of a quarter
of an hour, fenced-in lives, exceptions
and rules, encircled troops. He is one
with his desires. The horizon line of that moment
will never cross the light again, not its
intersections nor frontiers, not in the earth
where his body will transform into mole blood
and roots.

2

Almond trees are espaliered on either side
of the twisting road. Behind boxed hedges,
the garden withdraws into a trance of fragrances.
But once inside the house, these languors stop.

The maid dusts, mops, sweeps, plumps up pillows
whose slips are tatted with ivory lace.
Cousins assist in the delivery
with cool, damp cloths, a whiff of camphor and lilac
cologne. Birth is women's work, they say.
My mother in summer needs no coaxing to arrive
in the afternoon's aroma of lavender and mint,
fresh linen sheets. She takes the soft, white
contours as her due, a natural state
in the center of her wants. On the veranda,
the household's former only child
spills lemon tea on her pinafore.
"Where is papa?" she sobs and wipes her nose
with the back of her hand. Under the blue glaze of sky
the men are away in the towns buying and selling
olives and wine.
Their ancestors, gazing out of oval frames,
seem to bask in a glow of calm days.
Slow hours. Peeping through a frill,
my grandmother's nipple trickles milk the baby sips,
transfixed. This episode's horizon line wavers
and a powdered ash of roses sifts and blows into snow.

3
Snow melts on a clock's face whose hands
advance with the light of stars. In a climate
spared extremes, snow is a rare visitor and
leaves nothing but a tracery of loosely
remembered days in fading frames. Does my
mother remember the buttons she undid,
one by one, when she counted contractions and
her time had come? Does she recall the sky, white
as the chart and certificate that recorded

my birth? When I was born my mother prayed
I would be pardoned for giving testimony
to her intense desire. Mary, Mother of God,
was her mother then, blessed among women,
the one she called to when I pushed my way
out of her womb into an unwed mother's ward.

Snow, the boundary point of some far off
event dissolving when the owl roosted
in the cedar, its castings of mouse hair
and bones, gray pellets of dust on the ground,
snow dimming the light in chapel when I knew
the feel of smudged rosaries, four taps
on my body, the sign of the cross, professing
faith in Our Father, God, Mary, Mother of God,
Son and a Holy Ghost I could not find
in corridors where I stepped in unison, a child
in uniform engaged in small wars lost against
touching myself, wrong intent, glib speech.
Slowly, I learned to say what I thought
all wanted to hear: *mea culpa*, I regret
not being pure under a snow of bloomers and bibs,
cowls and flannel gowns flapping on a line
drawn against clouds whose edges blur and drift
in a fog of childhood rituals.

4
Belgium offers up its miles of plateaus,
polders, rivers, exhausted veins of coal
in the Borinage, and in the Ardennes, limestone
cliffs and wooded hills. On the outskirts

of Brussels, in the province of Brabant,
shrubs squat in a land whose horizon line
refused to disappear. My parents have vanished
to live elsewhere at opposite ends of continents.
I ask the nuns for them but no one says they
will never arrive nor why they should shift
their lives around. When my father dies, I am not
told. Did Mother Superior know? One day
holds another in its nest. Spring. Summer. Fall.

Dry snow falls on a skating rink where the wards
have come to scrawl their clumsy penmanship on ice.
I glide beyond the calls to form a line and leave.
Shifting limits, turns and frames. In a province
of lost origins where borders fold one into another
and trail off, the child I tap on the shoulder
turns to me with my own face and we know
we will escape the custody of the past,
giving astonishment a horizon line not yet
defined but waiting to be drawn.

WITHOUT TOYS AT THE HOME

No dolls, nuns thought we would
quarrel, no spinning tops, tin
what-have-yous, wind-ups, anything
which might distract offsprings
of the solemn church. Nuns meant
well as did their priests mumbling
over games of chess.

At the Home, I gave my fingernails names
and jobs: old thumb, Pierre, the cop,
pinkie Francine, slim-hipped one-note
pianist.

In my palms I loved the roads
that led me to my realms: Lantasah, high
in the reaches of Ti, Whoa and Neigh,
crofts for my shires, stallions and nags.

The rocking horse I wanted lived in a yellow
book where a boy arranged trains
on the floor. His sister held a china doll
with lambswool yellow hair. I let my playstone
sleep in the doll's chiffonnier,
in a velvet-lined drawer.

At the Home, our beds used to float like yachts
in the waves of our sleep. My sheet was a sail,
the pillow, a horse I rode calling to my second
finger, Dulce: "Stay away, nuns will find us
in my cloud."

A cloud won't stay put. More than once I've
been found out. My cheeks still smart from
being caught. Spring clouds, war clouds,
summer thunder, lulls and calms. Behind the gate
of the Home, the children have fallen in a mumble
of years, and their children have toys enough
to break, and their children enough for quarreling.

ESCAPE FROM THE IRON GATES

When we squatted by a puddle and wrote our names
on water with a stick, you curved "n" twice. Anne.
I crossed my "t's" as they rose.
The reflected sky trembled with our signatures.

Our angels were white clouds on the pond.
Their shadows trailed us and the winged caps of nuns.
How would we ride through the iron gates?
You wished for a donkey like the beast our Lord rode
in Jerusalem. Rather a white charger, I thought,
fit for a lady.

At night I rode my white pillow, moved my thighs
against its flanks in that damp, half-sleep the children
pulled over themselves like a coverlet.

Scrubbed nuns' faces in white cowls. Like moons they gleamed
at the end of long lines we formed to pray and study God.
No mirrors allowed. Anne, you searched for your face in the tops
of shoes. I greeted mine at the bottom of a bowl. Clutching our
rosaries, we kissed The Virgin's stony lips. Did she read my
carnal thoughts?

Angels still trumpet over Belgian fields. Years dart like birds
in and out of gates we have learned to open and to lock.
Surely, three-way, hand, full-length mirrors have not cracked
nor clouded over in rooms with our pillows and books, writings
and monograms on linen.

Somewhere, you arrange your blond hair into a cloud.
I shall never see your face again when I look into the water.
Your name's one syllable vanished with each letter's stroke.
Anne, shadowy-pale.

White pillow, our childhood on a ship, snowdeep by the pond.
My impure longings. The old disgrace brushes my face awake.

SETTING OUT FROM THE LOWLANDS

Do buildings in America grow taller
than Saint Julian's?
What will eat you when you drown?
The questions swirled
as the gate unlocked,
and hungry to be noticed
in my new, red dress,
embroidered flowers at the gathered neck,
I left them in the afternoon,
a child singled out for departure
at the start of the war,
before tanks
bulldozed the Do Not Trespass signs
in the capital.

Nuns in black and white,
children in weekday brown
waved me goodbye. Birdsong Street,
Brussels, Belgium, farewell.
"Come see us when you're a fine lady,"
a child blew a kiss
that flew over paths
straight as the rule of nuns
who kept us in line for the Liturgy
of the Eucharist, Midday Prayer,
the daily chanting at Evensong.

Who would eat my morning gruel,
sing my praise to God at Lauds?
What kept the ship afloat?
A great fish? I expected no less
than such miracles.

In America I have made the sign
of the cross in buildings
taller than Saint Julian's
and sailed into years
beyond that child's imagining
of a fine lady come back to gloat
in the Children's Home
whose corridors caught echoes
from small, red mouths
that set whispers afloat,
calling "pray for us, pray for us."

THE DREAM FOREST

The photo shows a backdrop of roaring falls and a plain child
who stands wary of the railing against which she leans.
Will it give way to an abyss billowing up plumes
of white horsetails? Will she stroke the fur of creatures
in a dreamforest where she loses who she is, a child
among people not wanting her reflection in their mirror?

"She stands there and gawks at their door," thin grandmother
nibbles melba toast. "Too late to send her back with the war
going on," fat grandmother pours cream on her shredded wheat.

"Did you see those pictures?" Thin grandmother notes
the harried faces of her son and his wife who'd gone all day
without a drink. "And this one of the child in front
of the falls? Look how she scowls."

"They had no business taking her," fat grandmother thinks
of the silver cocktail shaker reflecting her daughter's
manicure, her perfect clothes. "The child's a mistake,"
the women nod in rare accord.

In the same room, the child gobbles waxy American toast.
She's learned a language of turned backs, locked doors,
but not the trick of English words
which loop from mouth to mouth like moths,
maps on their wings she can't yet read
in the same way she is baffled by small print
on a matchbox, or the wrapper on a loaf of Silvercup.

She decides she will speak to the Moon of the Shambling Bear.
In her dreamforest. He will command: Mirror, show four
trapped bodies in the flames, toast-colored horses to pull
the hearse to and from the funeral. And show our girl
full-length, beautiful and cold, so rich in words,
she will fling them one by one into the roaring falls.

THE HAPPY CHILD

No one needs write HEAVEN in fluffed
white lines above the perfect town
her parents gave her
when she wanted a school
and regular bells.

Recently, white alphabets have entered
her house through front and back doors.
They tell her what to keep
like the fragrances of things
gone on before: cut hay, cake,
rain on wool sleeves.

This happy child leaping through hours
that end in a mist
of kisses her grateful parents give,
whatever she dreams

she will wake in a scented bed
to a day like any other welcoming
her breath, new words, the light steps she takes
to run after moths, filaments of webs, the circling
shadow of a hawk...

but she cannot die like the unhappy child
waiting for rescue,
its mouth at the bottom of the well.
She can never be that urchin hurting
in the cramped, cool dark,
spewing up furious words
everyone ignores.

SEASONS OF THE WAR

(for foster mother, Ruth)

In the foggy spring of the far off war,
what could I have given her?
A wind-up doll instead of the child
the doctor told her might cure pinched
nerves, migraines, a fraying marriage
of fifteen years. What did she want?

I wanted her amber pomade, lip balm,
lotions and lilac cologne, little jars
of rouge, vanishing creams, the lie
of "you are beautiful."

In the summer of the war,
on our porch with the blue glider
and white wicker chairs, what did she want?
Another start? Another drink? A body
not tricking her with blissful dreams
of mothering?

I longed to step into her paisley dress
with the fringed epaulets, to button
her yellow silk blouse, black birds on it.
I wanted them to fly out of her small breasts,
to sing to us in the morning.

In the stormy fall of the year,
I found her naked body in the hall.
"One too many," someone said. I'd seen the shot
glasses lined up on the bar downstairs
where she sat on a stool that spun
like a record on a phonograph.

Rhumba tunes pulsed softly
when she convalesced. In her peach robe
and matching bandeau pulling back her hair,
how fragile she was and inconsolable.

I envied her cream of tomato soup,
orange pekoe tea, the red lacquered tray
with parasols stenciled in gold.
They were close to her.

"What can I do?" I wanted to run to the store for her.
"Go comb your hair," I was dismissed.
She'd return to exposés in True Confessions,
Silver Screen.

I stole her tortoise shell mirror,
her apple green comb
in the winter when F.D.R. declared war.
She huddled by the radio,
sipping double scotches, straight.
"My nerves are raw," she'd sigh
and drape a hand across her eyes.
I learned to tiptoe up the stairs.

The war streaked headlines, dark bands
of birds, flying in a line.
Spring came. Summer. One day
she didn't answer to her name.

I thought I could have caught her last breath
in the tortoise shell mirror,
parted her hair with the apple green comb.

She was laid out in a beige
lace gown, lavender sash, her face,
a peaceful mask, but I stood by the casket
in a pink, puffed dress and choked back rage
as if it were a bone stuck in my throat.

Later, alone in her room, I did a rhumba
with her empty clothes, held on to the sleeves,
imagined her soul lolling on the deck
of a Caribbean party boat.
And I combed and combed my hair.

RAY

Ray, the seller of silks from Chicago,
did the mambo, the foxtrot, the rhumba,
the samba, the conga.
Narrow feet in silk-blend socks, two-toned
shoes. Slim, in flannel slacks, tapered shirts,
all of him sashayed and twirled.
He didn't miss a step. A smooth man.
Confident

except when his hands danced the hangover shake,
and he blinked back dreams
of tapping spiders with jittery legs
dangling from a web.

Ray, the seller of silks.
A bolt of crepe de chine, madame, he said
as he winked with a sweep of his hand
to conjure up grand distances
where women lounged on ottomans
and a man had only to point.
Ray from Chicago.

And he loved a well-turned ankle, seamed hose,
women who floated on clouds of perfume.
After closing the sale, he smoothed his hair
in the mirror and hummed

except when his mouth burned for a shot
of rye, bourbon, neat, whiskey straight,
the blackout cocktails of oblivion.

He had *boozitis nervosa*,
an inflamed need for one down the hatch,
another for the road, a little pick me up
and on and on. Bad nerves.

Ray, the seller of shantung, pongee, peau de soie.
"The best for the best," he told his customers,
opening the sample book.
The bosses agreed that Ray was number one,
born for the job.
Yes, he liked a drink, no sourfaced teetotaler,
not Ray.

But when he mixed bicarb and raw eggs,
lemon and cayenne to swig in one gulp at seven a.m.,
Ray did the tremble step, the morning-after shuffle.
In a pure silk robe, toting up the sales, he began
to forget stops to make, calls to return.
Ray, a blurred man, slurring his words, missing the beat,
headed for the drying-out tank jamboree,
the nightmare delirium hop.

WHAT ARE THE DAYS?

They are pilferers
stealing our resolve,
Thomas broods aloud.

Or stones
to use for good or ill,
says James sitting
on a rock with Peter.

Soon, the dreamer
comes along saying:
all days are brothers.

Aren't days fish
swimming to shore?
asks Simon, the fisherman
mending his nets.

They are coins to hoard
or to spend, Judas frowns,
and looks at his palms.

Twaddle, says Martha
running to fix supper.
You talkers, get me a hen,
get me an egg.

I bet you think
all the days are women
pouring wine and honey.

They are what they are,
says the hammerer of nails,
securing thieves
and the dreamer to the cross,
nothing more.

Sequences, Autumn, Meditations, Tu Fu.
I read "a hundred years of the saddest news"
and "the forlorn boat, once and for all
tethers my homeward thoughts."

In the halflight of the booth,
thoughts sputter and leap. My fears are cast
to drift on a raft of words.
When will he arrive? Why is he late?
Reasons gather and disband.

Chang-an has dropped off the cliff
of a thousand years into powdery stones.
Stumps of memory grow in a weed-ridden garden.
The beautiful girls do not gather
kingfisher plumes as gifts
in the China of Deng Xiaoping.

Who will write we lived in a glorious age?
Where are the banners of Emperor Wu?
Tatters in the earth and under the stars
of The Seated Ministers
or placed on graves at the Festival of Tombs.

"Chanting, peering into the distance,
in anguish my white hair droops."
So Tu Fu ends his meditations,
the ones he wrote at K'uei-Chou in Seven Sixty-Six,
his second autumn in the region.

After I put the sequences away,
my attention narrows on a mirror image of myself

grown old, white-haired, waiting for my husband.
Suddenly, out of a shadowy corner, he appears
with a story of confusion and delay.
We kiss. It is our twentieth autumn in the city.

SKYMYTHS

The six wives who ate onions are there
and the husbands who shoved them out of the hut,
long-haired Chasa arranges dew on stones and grass
for Chacaputi and his son, Topa.
The Tupi stargod, Maire-Monan, and one so large
the Zuni say his body can't be seen whole,
for his head sits in the west
while his heart beats at midheaven,
they are all there
reflected in the waters of the world,
in my bowl of facts, above our bluegreen ball
which will pass from vapor to ash
played by invisible lords of fate. They are there
in the trail of cornmeal drippings from the mouth of the dog,
in what Cherokee say of the Milky Way, the galaxy
the Yokut believe is dust from the race between antelope
and deer, a track made by snowshoes of a raven, the Inuit sing,
and the Fox's river of stars that sails above me, I, a person
of my tribe traveling from fire to fire, a wife,
onions on my tongue and a long mouth for speech.

WINTER MODES

What rose from those fallen days?
Tricks of light the ancients construed
as proof of doom or bliss.
We slept beneath the whale of night
and dreamed seven blue eggs
in The Pleiades would hatch blue fire
or damsel fish in a coral reef.

You said the saline level of primordial waters
was a quotient in our blood.
I tasted salt on your tongue.

Summer tides. The silver play of waves
whispered syllables of fish, sighs of lost
turtle years in underwater groves.
And inky clouds, the squids' defense
against insomniacal sharks.

In the jack pine, sparrows and jays
said who they were by their call.
Speedwell, lobelia grew in meadows we trailed.
We danced from happiness on the path to the sea
in that first summer of gazing at the Perseids,
of feeding anemones in the island rock pool.

Years later in winter, I ask if the nature
of snowflakes is known. You say temperature,
moisture, wind defines what transforms,
the single-planed, six-sided forms, not one
resembling the other since snow began.
You've gathered facts in a bouquet.

I ask you to look through the keyhole
to threadbare winters of another love.
Ragged snow, bridal lace. My fingers are almost blue
with cold on the January night I curse St. Agnes
for blessing my first union. When did I drop
the gold band in the sea?

Was it in summer? The residue of blasted stars
dims in my recollection of hungers and desires
before we married in July on the feast of St. Anne.
And in a union of circles moving towards their core,
I hold you fast, my love,
under the thorns of a red heaven
blooming planets and stars.

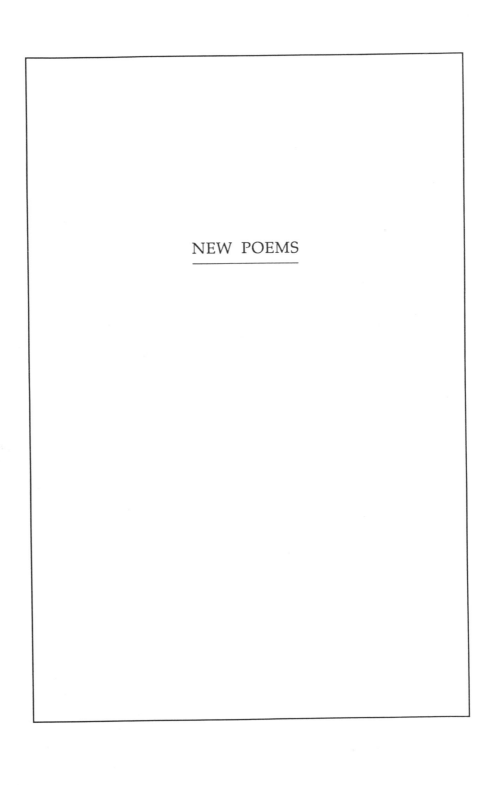

NEW POEMS

BELGIAN FLICKS

When I notice a mention of Belgian flicks
at MOMA, I start to remember bits of my
childhood in Belgium. Looking at the Flemish
Een Vrouw Tuessen Hand En Wolf, I know it doesn't
mean "a woman's hand tousled the wolf." The translation
(in parentheses) reads: "Woman in a Twilight Garden."

I used to genuflect to bells in Belgium
twice a day, at twilight and dawn in The Children's Home.
Cunning and alert, the nuns, I like to imagine, ran
in packs through the corridors bawling our names
Colette, Chantal, Jean-Marc, Pierre.

Another listed flick, *Het Kwade Oog*
reads like "I had a quiet egg" but means "Evil Eye."

What a hard time I had as a child wrapping my tongue
around Flemish words. The egg served up to me
once a week gushed a phlegmy yellow which I sucked
under the eyeful watch of a postulant
who had forfeited double features for the love
of God in Belgium. All the nuns spoke Wallonian,
Belgian French. Flemish was the language
of the poultryman and the seller of eggs.

At MOMA, the only film listed in French
is *Au Bout Des Lèvres* ("At the Tip of the Tongue").
"About Day Leavers" and "A Bootless Delivery"

seem too easy, but I revel in the thought
of "An Oboe on the Lever" with its image of music
and mechanical advantages.

Sisters believed we would wrangle over toy harmonicas,
ukeleles, flutes. I made harmony with my forefinger
pressed to the rim of a water glass,
and drew effigies of nuns drawn into dirt
with a crucifix or stick.

Other possibilities occur: lovers,
louvres, lavers, livers. I lived eight years or more
with the Catholic Sisters in Belgium
and never saw a movie.

GETTING UNDER WAY

Although she cannot draw numbers
on the waves with a twig,
at sea the ship is her earth,
not the small realm
of children where she had drawn water
from a tap, asked for time
which no one had.

Now crossing waters that clash
and contend with the wind, she gauges
her days to bells, compasses and pendulums.

The ship is getting under way.
A Mandarin orange on a pewter tray
is borne aloft in corridors.
Auburn light strikes high notes
on brass particulars. Ship's fittings,
buttons on the girl's spring coat
whose blue is a word she will grasp
as if it were a rail.

On a rolling ship, in a snug blue hat,
the girl feeds crumbs to the gulls.
On biscuit-colored velum in the Writing Room,
she scratches a message to her friend.
If she curls it into a bottle,
casts it to the waves, where will it drift?

Towards an absence in which her teachers
call the roll, to where she is not
leaning forward in a nailed down chair,
to a silence she will learn to fill
when she says clock and calendar,
not *horloge et calandre.*

Sounds formed by tongue and lips are thick
with the memory of everyday words
her friend will spout like a kettle of water
bubbling on the stove for chamomile tea
when the message comes ashore.

(My first years, and those of Belgian painter, James Ensor's last, quickly slipped by in Belgium.)

James Ensor Speaks of Colors and the Stormy Reception That Greeted His Work

"My colors are purified...integral and personal. Yet I upset convention...I was called nasty, bad...a simple cabbage became obscene; my placid interiors...hotbeds of revolution. Critics...snarled without let up...."

I Speak of Birdsong Street, of My Beginnings

On the Rue Chants D'Oiseaux, I warbled Sanctus from a small rose mouth. Puny recruit in the militant church, my blue uniform drew motes of silver dust, gray lint, yellow pollen from trees in a spring Brussels doled out as a gift to each inhabitant.

Love child, bundled off to the Catholic sisters, over the years I spooned simple cabbage in soups and stews without letup, sniffed nasty and agreeable smells in placid interiors. Lilacs and farts. Garlic and apples.

My walls were the grey white of fog-edged skies in autumn, of oyster shells, and rows of iron beds planting shadows like columns in an underwater light. Fumbling for a chamber pot in the dark, I smelled the waters of my body. When I rolled out from a flannel bolt of dreams, what was real? Piss that streamed in a roar. Like a waterfall.

James Ensor Writes of His Painting, "The Consoling Virgin"

"I had a glimpse of the Consoling Virgin...recorded her peaceful features on a panel of good quality. I kissed her little feet of snow and mother-of-pearl. On the hard substance of the old panel, the diaphanous image can still be made out..."

I Describe the Holy Mother and Reflect on My Parents

Stained glass windows beckoned me to begin such reveries as I could draw out of my body at matins, vespers and lauds. Snowy lamb of God lulled by Vierge Marie, who attended my prayers, a blue cloak falling to her feet. If she is the mother of God, God and Jesus are brothers. I asked but no one answered me. The God I believed in saw me squat on the toilet, a pimple on my rump, snot in my mouth. Didn't Sister say he was everywhere at once? Integral and personal?

Did my mother wear pearls? Did my father work the clasp to slip them off her neck? Before I was born my father kissed her little feet. Perhaps. My parents were diaphanous images. Yet I waited for them to shelter me, prayed they would come when I sang French words. *Fleur-de-lis* and *alouette*.

James Ensor Writes About Words

"Ah, but I love to draw beautiful words, like trumpets of light...words in the steel-blue color of certain insects, words with the scent of vibrant silks, subtle words of fragrant roses and seaweed...words whispered by fishes in the pink ears of shells..."

I Leave Belgium for Another Country

When I quit Brussels in the spring just before the war,
sailed past Ensor strolling on the beach at Ostend, my
words adored the ship coaxing me to America on the
steel-blue waters of the sea. Fishes sang green and orange
notes in my ear without reasons. Explorations. I will learn
of my dead father's holy words, the rain of gray words in
my mother's letters will bathe me in cool weather.

James Ensor in His "Reflection on Art"

"Our vision is modified as we observe. The first vision... is
the simple line, unadorned, unconcerned with color. The
second stage is when the better-trained eye discerns
values of the tones, their subtleties and play of light..."

Colette Inez in Her Reflections on Memory

The simple lines of trees on the Rue Chants D'Oiseaux, the
parallel lines of trolley tracks. The Children's Home. The
shadow of the iron gate. Where did they go? To the
heaven
of seaweed and roses Ensor gathered in plays of light?
And the child I was asks: what am I to learn in the subtle
world? And I answer her, to draw consoling words out of
the air. To arrange them like irises in a vase, to weave
them into proof our lives like a sea teem with
remembrances. To endure. Integral and personal.

Letters of the Great Artists, from Blake to Pollack, Random House, 1963, pp 174-177,
Ensor's translator: Paul Haesaerts

BAYSCENES, CHILDHOOD

1.

Let me point out a fat brown dog
and small Mrs. Foy.
Her baby squalls at the little waves.
A neighbor's tall child, I shoo off
the flies. There are plum jelly
sandwiches, wax paper and twine
before men level the fisherman's house.

2.

Why is no one on the sand?
Hasn't Mrs. Foy married the rolypoly
man who wanted things neat as a pin?
Her baby doesn't look like him
when she wheels it in a pram.
Their rooms lie silent in another time.
There goes my chance to save the twine.

3.

At the curve of the bay
there are troughs between the waves
and sand. Horseflies in the reeds blotch
my wet skin. The light has caught
the fisherman's house. The fisherman's
house is gone. Let me point out a ball
of twine unravelling and a thin brown dog.

4.

Who is looking at the sea? Not the dowser
nor the master of eels.
An arthritic dog blinks at the waves,
tracing a cry's missing body in the foam.
Somebody's child stares up like a fish
from the dregs of the bay.

5.

Explainer of hours, philosophers,
why aren't we seals?
I admit to a love of balancing, and propose
such things as are circular: wrasse in the crevices,
scallops in the littoral of burrowing clams
who only see the world
circumscribed by tides, helpless at the last.

FOSTER MOTHER DEE'S DEPARTURE

What did she do after she dumped Ray
and left the stucco house
with the tomato red stoop?
Hennaed hair in a purple snood,
black lacquered toenails in open-toed shoes.
Had another Cuba Libre, Singapore Sling.

When she lived with us, snow choked the lawn,
a few birds sang, rain released the snow
whose white I linked in memory to a ski suit
she didn't wear for skiing. Get me a drink,
she'd command, tossing her gloves
on the floor, baring teeth

that could tear the flesh of young dogs
as she roved through swamps, howled in the woods
near school and church. But when she'd leap
in my room, scream, bruise my throat,
her hot breath in my face like a javelin,
I prayed for a magic stone
to make her disappear.

Dandelions seeded the lawn.
Winds blew. Tiger lilies. Lion rays of the sun
pierced her dark room. What did she do in bed
benumbed with Jim Beam,
hunched with Lord Calvert? What did Ray say?
Did he plead with her to stay or leave?

The windows saw the last
of her scowls as she blurted out her hatred
of flowers, and birds
excluding Four Roses, barring Black Crow.

One night racing past the house,
she saw me on the stoop. And Ray, naked
on his knees begging for clemency
from the gods of booze. I rubbed a stone
flung down from the trees. Ray became a passing
cloud, Dee, a pool of gin polluting the lawn,
clogged with damp leaves.

Sometimes I thought I might
gasp my last breath at N.Y. Tel.,
but went on intoning
the lion is busy, please call again.
Plugged into a board,
headset snapped over my ears,
to drunks, cracked voices on the line,
to anyone possessed of a dime,
I asked: "your number, please,"
again and again.
A supervisor had told me:
"rhyme nine with lion,
five with die of."
The first year I lived
on my own, learned to please men
without getting undressed,
checked out books
from the library: *Anna Karenina*
and *House of the Dead*, I swallowed
two bottles of Anacin but groggily woke
in my rooming house to turn eighteen.
The next night on the job,
I ripped the cords
out by their stems, left them
in a tangled heap, imagined lips
shouting: "operator, operator,
I've been cut off,"
across the local wires
and into my last hour of taking calls
in the island towns.

THE BEQUEST

My saint protected dreamers and fools.
I almost heard her clicking tongue,
saw her eyes roll heavenward
when uninvited I left to bathe in the scent
of my mother's roses, smokey violets and ferns.
Those days that lead to her
blue-shuttered house were mine to inherit.

Awarded dark purple lilacs
and a stand of cypresses, flame-shaped,
replicating those in the calendar
of Duc de Berry, I came into clouds
of mimosa, hills and twisting roads.
My legacy: cobbled streets, medieval walls
in a town where I stumbled
on angels, unicorns and the Virgin Mother
in perfect stone.

I beseeched the saint of sun-bleached
nightclothes inhabited by airy figures
in the wind. I prayed to the angel
of walkways and shrubs, of brooms
and iron furniture to bless the yards of France,
to hover over my mother's house.
She was there, frail behind the window.
Lift her from the chair, float her to the door,

I implored, and the door opened
to the secret daughter
she gave away to the Sisters,
the child named after a martyr and saint,
but neither one nor the other,
it opened to me, a woman
offered a cool entreaty into her mother's rooms
and the gift of a crucifix, my bequest.

RIVER HOUSE INVENTIONS

Blistered hands raw on the oars,
I row past her house, call out her name
or

sailing past the river house,
I wave to the woman on the dock.
She crochets memories
she will throw over her lap.

Anchored to childhood, moored
to old age, she rocks in her chair,
watches the river
turn into a cloud the shape of a girl reading a book.

But I can annihilate the boat, make the river
disappear, plant the house on a plateau or a hill.
I can have the woman on the dock look out
through French windows at the river and sky,
make her believe in the power of prayer.

I can re-invent my parentage. Not father-priest,
but father-baker, hair the color of daily bread.
Not mother-archivist, but mother-sailor-with-a-crew
steering a course for the Argentine.

In a limousine I may carry a cone of roses,
and a book of common prayer, want to say
"I am your daughter,"
but do not when she floats to the door.

Spectral woman, she beckons me into her house,
unties the cord, cuts the roses on a slant,
slips them in a milkglass vase.

She looks at me when I look elsewhere.
I look at her, her milk white hair.
In the vestibule mirror
she is what I might be and am not.

But if I push the boat back into the river, pull
on the oars, fashion myself into a girl struggling to sail,
calling out to be seen, then what?
What has gone on between the woman and her child?

"Curious," she might say to a visitor, a priest
come to share church talk and a cup of tea. "I saw a girl
wave to me from a boat. She called out my name.
It was no one I knew." How very odd, they will agree.

This is true. A proper daughter in a proper suit, I knock
at her door for the second time in thirty years.
We nod, pump hands, say where we've been.
I don't know who she is and will not know even after death
strolls up from the river to take her in his arms.

And she will not know I have become
a visible woman, full of inventions.

Lemon trees in a garden. Portola Valley. My father arrives, a priest on the hill come to say Mass. His horse has galloped down Sunday miles to Santa Clara, San Jose. The great earthquake is fresh in the memory of those who kneel among redwoods at Our Lady of Wayside.

He will blink when he sees my mother's owl eyes, gold, her lank hair. She will press her lips to his bald pate, trace thin shadows under eyes that squint late into the night correcting proofs of treatises. They do not know I am watching them, that I will be steeped in their stories, stirring my image at the edge of a pond.

When she dances in a hobbled skirt, she circles towards him, her head turning this way and that. He looks the other way, then takes her in his hungry gaze. Lichen on the oaks, a cloudy net of snow scrolled over the forest. Red crossbill and tanager sing a mutter of notes when he snaps off his collar.

In a pool of sunlight, she brushes away scratchings of pine duff and twigs, clips back a fall of hair with a tortoise shell barrette. To have rescued him from paid women is no small thing. "Ma chère, what are you staring at?" he asks, wiping mist from his spectacles. She points to a salamander migrating from rocks to the stream. Its tawny color like faded tiles in Gascony, or the palm of her flame-shaped hand smooth against his lips. Shuddering, he sees her head bowed at Mass, a tatter of lace draped on her hair. She will swallow the Host he rests on her tongue. She cannot see me kneeling. Even when I wave, I am invisible to him.

Now I stand near the water that touched their bodies when they swam. Woodland scents of eucalyptus and loam. Spring again. Drumming thunder. A red camellia is blown from its stem by the wind. Its damp face on stone lies ruffled upward to a thumb of coruscating sun barred by rain.

So lies my paralyzed mother in the house where she was born along the Garonne. Outside her gate, I was no one she saw. So rests my father under his marker blessed by the charity of time. Spared the choking collar, he might have called me daughter.

Their lives glimmer in my narrative like worlds of more than one moon, not Jupiter's thirteen, but the Martian Dimos and Phobos, a pair to survey, my distant parents circling gardens of intricate light.

SEINE-ET-OISE

Umber, ocher, linden, oak
leaves circling
with French phrases beyond the line
of my clenched smile
targeted by the camera's lens.
As I bantered with a boy,
someone posed us.
My back was turned in the next shot
of the palace,
its pink and cream stone.

When I gazed at the facade
overlooking the gardens,
I heard water-music bubble up like fireworks
breaking into smoky clouds.
And from the set edge of a narrow mouth,
his voice correcting me.
"You meant Lully not Lalo."
"Exactly so. Je vous remercie."
I lowered my eyes.

Twenty years before that pose
at Seine-et-Oise, before I studied rules
of etiquette in the reign of Louis XVI,
that boy's parents in spring,
mine in fall, huffed on beds
that dimpled with each moan and turn.

So briefly guests of history,
exalting France, they kneeled at her monuments.
We did as well, prattling about Molière, Racine,
of Marie Antoinette's
silliness at court,
her grace and calm under the blade
of the guillotine.

CONSPICUOUS ABILITY IN LITERATURE
COUNTS FOR LITTLE IN THE JOY OF HUMPING

1

Virgin's Row
Chaucer's nun in wimple and beads
wasn't helped by a knowledge of French
(spotty, at that)
and collapsed intact
with her little white thighs
on speaking terms with the Bishop of Death.
(Mon Dieu, Mon Seigneur)

Emily's catafalque burdened with assonance
as the body rode its meters to the ground.
Scarce alignments with her lust,
no adjustments possible.
(Ma Soeur de Poésie)

2

Burning Polaris in the northern sky
writes its lines for a ship
caught in a warp of my figurative speech.

3

O Red Baron in your Fokker,
flying satyr, the fuel is low.
Your machine refuses the simplest signature,
any complimentary close for the Endowment Winner.

Conspicuous ability! I'm falling into desuetude,
an exhausted wasp clinging to the light
of a drifting sun.

4
Militant wind, blow
your mouth-to-mouth resuscitation.
My gibbering heart reads a silence
it wants to translate to a name
that lives now down beneath Polaris
and rings and rings its Lokme bells
like a high-pitched star on a 78
uncracked disc of perpetual song.
(Chanson d'un ange qui chant)
Lily Pons, mon amour.

GUARDING THE UNREVEALED

Red father, the sun who brought her fire
in the morning mourns the death of night.

Green mother, the moon who lit her books
at night mourns the death of day.

And I, the secret daughter, I mourn her.
The body of the past resides within me,

red, spectral, filled with convolutions,
whispers and cloudy codes.

Days fall on their knees like supplicants
commemorating loss. She destroyed all evidence

I was hers. There is nothing to know,
the gardener intones cutting lilies for the funeral.

Withholding my name, she did not hear bells
summoning worshippers to Mass.

Behind latched doors, she did not hear the call
for the priest and made no sign

of having heard The Last Rites.
She will enter her notion of heaven.

Squatting in the women's house
with tapes and notes,
the anthropologist asks
how they weave the cloth,
prepare the manioc,
what they think of the men's house
across the yard.

The anthropologist may not see
the men's house
nor the sacred flutes whose low notes
she will hear.
She is still a woman
to the chief who sits on the ground
and sharpens his spear.

Women must listen, they must not
see the flutes. When they die
they will not have seen them
nor the men's house. They will mend
hammocks and remember the woman
who dared in the far time,
how tribal rape was her punishment.

"Today," says the chief, "we will begin
the alligator ritual. Our arrows
will speak to us and our songs
will have names: Evening, Sadness,
Woman Demon."

The sun weaves the hair
of the questioner with gold.
She puts away her notes, rewinds
the tape. "Tell your people
we are not savages," says the chief,
looking straight on at a camera
whose magic he has just begun to grasp.

I will take the lawn into my recollection
of leaves, ginkgo, oak picked off by the wind.
The katydid's throb to be kept in a bowl
with a set of proper terms. Winter.

The children are going to far places
in the poem I will write after it snows.
Marigolds to fit into my description
of the town they leave in the summer.
Seasons in between? Trillium, spring,
asters, fall.

The children have come back from Germany
and France. I am writing the poem in which
they leave again for The Netherlands. Snow
on a path to the letterbox has melted away.
Here's a letter describing summer

in The Hague. Begonias, phlox. If I open
up a box of katydids, the terms won't change
how we say farewell. Best to go to Limousin
with grandiose plans; dinner with Lady Diana
in a vanilla confection of a dress. A surfeit
of lilies. Spring.

THE DANCE OF ADOLPH AND EVA

Roses on tombs, corsages of rain,
Russia's white sky and a mountain
of bones dead in the April
of Adolph and Eva when they danced

the Goosestep pavane.
A history of roses over the ages,
Rose buds in the Alpenwelt.
Rose-colored dust from shattered stone

as Adolph and Eva twirled in Berlin.
Victorious snow and defeated lines
writing decline in the uproar of wounds.
Eva, my bride. Adolph, I do.

The marriage vows to oblivion.
Her shot of doctored wine,
his gun explodes. On hind legs, Blondi,
the Fuhrer's dog dances for scraps

of Limburger cheese when that April
and stammering bees recalled the rose's
literature, a common feat of memory
in the library of hives.

MIRROR

Something looks back
each time I move.
O demon mask, sad, turned-down
mouth, simulacrum, watery-eyed
eater of bland or pulsing days,
doppelganger assembled
out of air and pure light
to burn away like fog.

You hollow out a face
as if I were mud.
You, sculptor, witch, vendor
of masks, is there nothing
when I leave, nothing
in vanity's house of fears
set loose in the dark?

When you sell the mask
to a buyer I can't see,
will it be the god without a face?
It, too, will fall when all
is withered by fire.
This truth is in my mouth,
the bite of my skeleton
grazing dust.

MAX IS ASKED TO REACH INTO THE PAST FOR MEMORIES

(for my father-in-law)

It's not like pictures in a book. This one. That one.
Suits on a rack. From a kid what do I remember?
I'm a boy. How old could I be? Rivington Street.
I buy and sell eggs. Later, I buy a horse.
Later, a store.

What do I remember?
Your Aunt Rosie says you should meet this girl.
What should I tell you?

So who knew what would happen?
Your mother hasn't got what to wear. I buy
her a coat. I take her to nice places to eat.
She picks at her food.
A quiet girl. I'm thirty already. She's twenty-three.

Such a wedding. For this I was in debt five years.
What else do I remember?
What do you want to know?

Sylvia has a dog she is crazy about but when
you're born she has to give it up. It will bite
the baby, she says. I shouldn't smoke, it's bad
for the baby, she says. When you were a kid,
we never went out. So then I left. Every week
I sent a check.

You want more? Listen, it's all right. You never
were hungry during the war. Remember, you'd come
to see me in my hotel. A smart boy, a good-looking kid.
What you wanted, I gave. Listen, your mother and me,
we couldn't get along.
I'm not in the phone book now. You couldn't look me up.
I'm out of style, an old man.
Your Aunt Rosie never forgets to call.
You want I should remember?
What should I remember?

MAYBE

Maybe I ought to ask him, Ed,
get that broom out of the closet,
as if he would do it,
I thought to myself,
as if that man would pick up one thing
in this house to help out.

Maybe I ought to sniff his shirts
for French perfume, look for telltale hairs.
He may be working overtime
on a red head or a blonde.

Maybe I ought to get a blowcut,
lose ten pounds, dress for success,
fly to Nevada, sue for divorce.

Maybe I ought to get a newspaper
to hide behind when Mr. Do Nothing
wants his eggs just so with medium toast,
light on the butter.

Maybe I'll run off tomorrow
with the salesman from Sears
who sold me the broom.
He looked like a sport, roguish eyes,
stuck out ears, though.
Maybe.

That's daughter, Orleen, in a tooled-leather frame;
she hustles hard in back street bars
way north of Nashville and the bus depot
where she hollered goodbye.
Brown, drowsy eyes and no money down,
funneling through hours, a streak of towns,
shut-down mills, courthouse lawns;
until the city slammed her awake
with Dixieland jazz and the trumpeter's ache
for riches and flesh.

December rain on the Natchez trail
Time beats down the path.
Mama's gray like the Natchez rain,
is sitting it out on an iron bed,
remembering Orleen, her last born child
singing gospel in the choir, nice-living times,
hoecakes in the oven and the ribs done brown,
mortgage-paid days before her man
and the farm went under,
and the world got older
like the old folks parlor
with its tacked-up sign:

GIVE THANKS TO THE LORD
FOR WE LIVE IN HIS PERFECT MERCY

RIVERWALK

Skipping blue stones
in the stream,
we watch
intersecting circles
furrow the mirrored clouds,
and near a slope
of moist leaves,
hear the frog's
courtship recital
abruptly muddled
in thunder and rain.

Under a sheltering ledge,
in a cave
our bodies find
their languages.
We are waterfalls
joined in descent.
We are green monkeys
howling in the delta,
buried maps
to the secret temple.

You want me as your river,
burrowed into land,
I want you as my bridge,
the brace
of your towers
and cables.

In the light
your lips barely move
when you say the sun will die,
girders rust, arches buckle,
piers rot. I shrug, blink.
Heat. Nothing stirs.
By the riverbank
black and purple stones
glisten as we stand.
I slip my hand into yours.
You hold on. Impending chaos
seems improbable.

SHAKING THE MAN AWAKE

When stars take their place
between trees,
she wagers on the dark
to do what it does
under a moon pillowed in clouds
like the man at her side.

He is a stranded seal, she thinks.
A moon of long bones
staggers through leaves.
She bets on it to fall under the earth,
for the god of seals to avenge her loss
of a husband to spirits.

In a dream she drops her winnings
where two crows sit at a gaming wheel.
Shaking the man awake, "Listen," she says
and takes his shoulders in her hands,
but it hardly seems right for her
in a world rolling the days like dice,
to carry on so much.

GLENN

There are tribes that would call him
a spirit orating at the whim of gods.
In a healing temple of the state,
he is speaking to the counselor
of names. "Hualpa, Capoc, the trial begins,"
he intones, gesturing to a crowd
of imaginary witnesses, his pale head
looking up for informants in the clouds.

When he is sad, he sees the forest harvested
by fire. "Cones of charred pine
lie in the ancient places. Chan Chan. Moche."
He rolls his eyes. He is Huascar, the prince,
he says to us.

At school, we recall, he loitered in halls
waiting to buttonhole someone for answers
to what is fiction, what is truth,
is death absolute?
At his mother's funeral, he thought
he saw her rise,
a white-robed woman, singing.

We remember his thin shadow on the quad,
the back pack crammed with books,
how he'd lean in on debates, life on other
galaxies, reason, faith. When he told us strobes
in his skull pulsed knowledge from the Inca world,

we called to him, come back, but he'd lost
his plain, short name, and spoke a dialect
of Quechua, he said. Sometimes he'd remember us,
our town, our school. "Spies," he confided
are in the labs filming crucial documents.

Except for a bed, a chair, a bureau, the room is bare.
Today, Glenn says, he will visit the Lord of the Condor.
He will kneel at his throne.
His pectorals will be in the form of the moon.
In the days to come he will live in the temple Coricanche,
in its golden enclosure.
A woman in a white robe will sing to him
in the ancient places of the sun and moon.

Only a few of us have come to see him off.
We wave goodbye.

THE RECLUSE

Miniature prints of the short-tailed shrew
appear on loose, fresh snow. Snow fleas
leap over buckets of maple sap.
First butterfly, the Mourning Cloak
shakes out its dreams of gales and ice.

Clouds like bass swim in a sky he scans
through binoculars. First, he spots a chicken hawk,
then on the ground, a dormouse sipping at a puddle's edge,
farther on, a black crowned heron in the willow root.
He fondles his fishing rod, reel, line and lure,
lands a speckled trout to grill for supper.

In a dream an ample woman climbs into his bed.
He wakes to bars of moonlight on the plumped up
pillow next to his. When he peers up at Cetus,
The Whale, disrupting the south with stars,
he imagines his past as a fish he reels into shore
and throws back.

Goldfinch twitter in the thistle patch.
Caterpillars feed at the mid-rib of the leaf.
He sits behind the yew hedge at the far end
of the porch and whittles a stick from limber ash.

The last of the bees hum in the asters.
Floating rafts of leaves sail on the pond.
Fish seek out hollows beneath the ice.
Night after night he envisions a woman
moaning and rolling in long, blue hours.

The logging roads fan out in pallid light.
At the snow hole's edge, something leaves
its print. Not a weasel. But a wolf-maiden,
a bear woman, a fox mother.
He squints at a sky reprised in the water.
He glances toward the roadbed
and two blue feathers rise where the hawk fed.

THE LEAVETAKING

(for Jenny)

She hides behind ferns on the veranda
until night numbs the house with sleep.
Wisteria, the child repeats a favorite word,
lets it whistle in her mouth.
Mother and father rattle doors
in the bruise-colored light of her dream.
She sees their shadows rear back
like trees in a storm or stallions
in a burning barn.
Now they are lions that jump through hoops
of fire. She holds the whip. The house
goes up in smoke. Her dolls are gobbled
in the hearth. They shout a language
in the flames no one decodes.
Ki o lay, chur wi...
The child wakes to birdsong at dawn.
"I will say one hundred words in French,
*café au lait, oiseau, nuage...*to France
on a plume of wind. See my arms?"
She flaps them for Feathers, her thrush
in a cage, but he takes no notice
of her rise over shrubs, trees, high over
the matchbox of a house where the parents
strike their heads against the wall,
flare and sputter out,
their shadows on the yard, exhausted moths,
then specks of ash.

When he rings her doorbell,
snow in no hurry to fall
fills the window
with pinwheels and harps,
angels and flutes.

"Don't you see dark tears
frozen in snow?"
She points to a sheet of notes
and brushes back her curls.
He is slim as a cadet.

Lighting the piano lamp,
he stares at a pastel
of Felix and Fanny Mendelssohn.
"I see a score of music," he says.
"Let's hear you play."

Later, loose waves of music
ripple like waters
in a rushing stream.
She is snared in the thunder
of octaves quaking on bass.

"Fortissimo...that passage again."
To turn a page his hand
swims up from his side
like a languorous fish.

Caught in a tide of song,
she learns by heart
the span of her pageturner's wrist,
the strand of wayward hair
he keeps smoothing into place.

"Don't you see notes like blackbirds
locked in flight?"
she flutters at the lesson's end.
"I see that practice makes mastery,"
he puts away the metronome,
slips on a dark coat, moves

out on gray scales of light,
to climb out of her field,
a fugitive note, a wooden soldier
detached from a box of toys.

To leave a pair of garden gloves
caked in the mulch, to let the spade
rust with the watering can
tipped over on its side
where the cucumber vine sprawled
star-shaped yellow flowers,
is no big thing,
doesn't need to be emphasized.

I don't think of them in the city
any more than I think of the doctor
or the hospital I used to call
for condition reports.
Death, which wavered in your room
tiptoed out, content
to wilt old roses in a bowl.

I'm used to not seeing roses clambering
on the trellis, to not catching
the stream of their scent,
have almost forgotten the cupboard
where I kept the white vase
to put them in, and the rooms
where I fretted alone,
weighing your cures and the cost.

At the end of an access road,
the house is absorbed in other ways
by people we don't know.
The moving van rattled our things.
Tureens, cadenzas, coasters
and frames. Nothing of great prize.

I want to emphasize you,
who'd slowly gained strength in the garden,
eating sun-warmed tomatoes, cucumber salad
with lemon and oil, eating brown bread and fish,
that you came away with me and you healed.

EARLY JUNE MEDITATION AT LAKESIDE

Fire alarms, a far off wail.
Fireflies twitch in the grass.
At summer's doorsill we stand,
a seasoned couple in good weather.
It seems no great matter a comet hurtles
towards the sun, that a child's
charred bones will slip into earth.

In the city the firemen
have put out the fire.
We are here and not there.
Look at the dream
we have: a field of mullein, a lake,
two flies trapped in a hub of silk.

This night belongs to an interpreter
of wasps, aphids
in the mouth of a ladybird beetle
carrying red spots
on the dark ground of her back.
We count her years by them,
we who have learned
to eye seconds on a watch,
to burn old calendars, accounts.

And this night belongs to the author
of fire in the arsonist's heart,
to comet tails and summer births
where frogs, and bugs
claim their brief patch of dark.

No one cares if we swim naked
in a lake whose fish gulp shadows
and trembling stars.

The child's mother will buy a casket
with money from the firemen.
Our throats are dry when we think
in summers to come
we will be red cinders
rising from a burning house.

OHIO LETTERS

Dear S.,
On my cutting board, tomato quarters
resemble the torn off ears
of an Aztec spirit.
The malevolent Tomatl.
I can't appease him with song.
Having yielded my voice
to the god of sore throats,
I'll offer him cheese,
gold as the jeweled pectorals
of a nobleman.

My meal, an open-face grilled cheddar
and tomato to devour alone
where the Lords of Ohio
whet their knives
for the sacrifice of the maidens.
On the south green
they scream as if it were time
for virgins to leap
into the hubbub of promises
for perpetual life.

My hunger for home rumbles like a summer storm.
I write you words, notes, poems, curved,
pressed hard against the page.

Dear S.

It's past the start of my tenure on a mountain
that holds small towns like a sow
nursing its litter.
West of Parkersburg, east of Chilicothe,
among wind and water gaps,
here I am in the Appalachian ranges,
and I dislike mountains,
stacked earth at the end of town streets.

Selling pressed dates on camel back, your ancestors
roved through deserts, mine foraged through plains.
You ask for my dream: a singer finds her voice
perched like a bird in the sycamore.
What does it mean? Tomatl lurks
on the outskirts of town,
readies his troops to clash against foes
in the roar of the stadium.
Silence is the penalty for loss.

O Dear S.,

Again I wake without you
and the air is sharp with memory,
the gentle routines of a seasoned pair.
In a tangle of purple berries and spiraling leaves
corn light fades into clouds
out of reach.

Peering up at constellations, I stumble past trees
that vault towards heaven's mountain.
My body wants to nourish poems at each teat
like a dazed pig, one eye half-opened,
wary as a bloodshot moon skulking out of her pen
behind the watchful mountain.

           Faithfully, C.

MIDWEST ALBAS

In heartland cafeterias, I hear
the resolute chirp of women
heaping pale food on white platters,
tuna surprise, baby corn niblets,
flash-frozen cod, potatoes
whipped, ridged, stuffed, mashed,
washed down with peach cobblers
coconut pie, sighing under vanilla
ice cream in a scoop,
and loaves, wafers, snaps, strips,
squares, puffs, crullers, cakes,
guests at the wedding of lemon
and meringue, at the marriage of brown
and serve, humming in the company of veal,
sole in foil baked by midwestern women
offering consolations of buttermilk
biscuits, the solace of fritters,
throughout the breadbasket states of the land,
rendered helpless in a rain of salt,
in a meltdown of cream.

THE BOY WHO LOVED WINTER

Not snow ebbing from the crèche
at Saint Perpetua, but snow packed down flat
as the sled he flopped on, his shouts
of pleasure bounding through the yard
where she would sunbathe in summer, the neighbor,
hot in a skintight suit, fanning herself
with a magazine, smoke from her cigarette
curling in the snowball bush.

In the boy's dream a snowman
clutching a broom, watches every move
of her hiked-up shoulders as she unhooks her bra,
how languorously she steps out of her underpants.
The snowman starts to melt.
Winter executioner, she lops off its head.

Rain. Mud. Bloated skies. Nervous birds
in and out of every shrub. Bugs.
The boy hates spring. His mother's rhododendron club,
Sunday dinners, asparagus and lamb after Mass.
Lent. What to give up? In confession,
he rattled off his sins, reading impure
comic strips, sneaking a look
at the paper next to his,
playing with himself.

He'll give up longing for snow, and forty days
of not peering through binoculars
at the woman next door.

He'll pray for her husband in the Merchant Marine,
an officer of forgettable looks, not like her,
whose eyes burn in a long, sharp face,
her body curved like hills of snow he longs to ride
stripped naked in winter.

THE BOY IN THE POOL

The chance look a boy throws out at me,
our eyes meeting in air smooth as water
above blue tiles paler than the sky.
Am I a woman like his mother?
No, I haven't given birth.
Does he see my face dissolving
in the locker mirror, chlorine in my eyes
and hair? Amber-haired, floating on his back,
kicking up foam, he seems to belong
to the horizon line where sky and water meet.
Soon he will feel the sun's hot kiss
on tight, brown skin. He may call up my face,
intent and strange to him in a dream tonight.
I am the woman he thought he knew,
the only witness to catch his double gainer
from the topmost board. Across the water,
I call him by name. Which have I chosen for this dream
he spins for us out of green air and light?
I think he is my son at summer's heart.
This scene is drawn in a northern country.
The lifeguard locks the pool gates.
A flickering moment and the boy packs
his knapsack for school. I stare at yellow leaves
gathering in an empty pool.

When she stopped running
she was a red boat
idle in the grass.
When she ran, the sun
drifted off course
behind a cloud.
Absent in the orchard,
with shipwrecked apples
she has rolled
into spirit worlds of fire.
I looked in vain for the red
of her hunter's coat,
in the spot
at the woodpecker's neck,
barberry shrubs
at the edge of the grove.
I could not find her
dangling from a bough,
as if she were
the fruit of the tree.
One day in a dream
of millipedes and snails,
and present among stones,
she will float towards me
on the path, my child
in a cloak of red leaves.

ADVICE TO A WRITER IMAGINING CONCEPTION AND BIRTH

Look for a tree stump in the woods. Compare it to love,
examine the particulars, how your mother mounted
your father on Labor Day in a bungalow, Liberty, New York.

Describe a snowfall before your parents met. Take your time.
Leave out myth and literature. Relate it to life in an American
town, one with a rotating cocktail lounge.

Now imagine yourself as a parchment worm
wedged into a crevice to avoid attack. Liken your fear
to a clamp. How does it resemble the opal clam

from New South Wales? Speak up. Check it out.
Write a poem of departure in which you use the color blue,
a hue like the glow of fish cast ashore by a stormy sea.

Your parents are leaving town. They've rented a bungalow
in Liberty, New York. You're not around to say: after dark,
exact change. You're not even a tiny moonlet in a microscope,

a bluet in the woods. Contrast your nothingness to words
that start with "k": killjoy, kisscurl, kelp. Are these words
comical in any special way? Say how you feel about kale.

Will you grow to leave it on your plate?
Your parents sit in a trance. They have just made love
and are counting snowflakes: uno, dos, tres...

Are they from Bogotá, Colombia, and in New York on
a whim? You are about to divide. Say something about the
intricate coil of DNA. Double helix. Double Dutch. Jump in.

Make the leap. Now you're a nation newly emerged.
Dispense with history, the transitory passions of people's wants.
Words are dropping fast.

LINES FOR EASTERN BLUEBIRDS

Not Maeterlinck's storybook
creatures twittering
happiness in Charleroi
birdbaths, not Snow White's birds
chirping when she mopped for the dwarfs,
but bluebirds contending
with starlings, sparrows,
swallows, wrens, clashing
in open country of scattered pines,
woods gashed by loggers and fire,
bluebirds seizing beetles, crickets
in loose snarls of grass,
roosting in orchards,
on high tension lines over back roads,
piping variations
in sloughed over double notes
where loosestrife flares against a sky
wanting no particular reply
to katydids' debate: do they burn
the same blue, the summer day,
did they, do they, learn blue, bluebird, jay?

ANIMAL BODIES IN VIRGINIA

Joe, the dog, howls in dry grass.
When I step out the door
he tilts his head, lets out
a short bark. I start to sprint
past fields. On either side cows graze
in black and white bodies.

Joe and I run hard. If racing's
what this is, I let him win.
But coming back from where he's gone,
he stands his ground like a palace guard,
indifferent to my calls: C'mon, Joe,
how about it, let's do it, let's go.

When I trot up the road, alone,
past shrubs, the empty pool, cows,
my breasts sway under my blouse.
I step into a child's body, chest,
hips, face, wind-resistent, lean. I grow.
My breasts are fondled in the dark,
soothed by the cushion fullness makes.

I climb into bones and fur.
I am Joe and yap in a glut of dull hours,
flop in the shade, streak in the field.
I flow back into my woman's
flesh. It accommodates snippets
and shreds of a spaniel's aspirations,
and also mine: to stay close
to what counts, to run with my own kind.

THE TRAPPER AND THE ARCTIC FOX

In outposts of Attapiskat
in farthest reaches of polar drifts,
natives say the arctic fox sleeps
with both eyes open, it is that difficult
to come upon it unawares.

The trapper looked for his wife
in the muskeg,
the bog of the tundra.

The soft bark of the fox
they say, may lead the hearer to guess
the animal is far away when close by.

The trapper looked for his wife
in the bear skin coat
she trimmed in ermine and rabbit skin.

Except for the thick, white pelt,
the arctic fox, handsome, a beguiler,
resembles his cousins to the south.

She left her husband when the fire was doused.
The sky in a trance, she met the fox.
His spirit life passed through her flesh.

Profiled in moonlight, mouse fur
and bloody owl feathers drooping
from his mouth, the fox will trail
the polar bear for droppings and scraps.

The trapper moaned when the Wolf Moon rose.
The woman he married slipped out of his bed
to run off with the fox.
She will never return

from the drift ice edge and gravelly fields
faintly lit by Fox-in-the-Sky, Vulpecula,
north of The Hare.

LOST LETTERS

Carted away to a dump in the sky,
the purloined letters
topple into slags of alphabets;
DICK's lost NE, PHONY deprived of SYM,
ASSY pried loose from EMB,
and split from ES, SEXHOUSE brazens it out alone
off the park.

In abecedarian space, the scramblers
pluck from the discards:
STAR reverts to RATS,
marquees of the night spell: COME TAX PREPARED
IN THE REAR, dubious signs in the year of the churl.

What will words say of the loss
when our lipreaders go numb,
one by one like neon towns whose fuse has blown?
In a mute void we will begin again with A mislaid from the tail
of LITTLE NICK'S PIZZ
or end on Z's fizzle to round out another alphabet.

BOOKS BY COLETTE INEZ

The Woman Who Loved Worms
Doubleday
1972
Carnegie Mellon University Press
Classic Contemporary Series
1992

Alive and Taking Names
Ohio University Press
1977, 1980

Eight Minutes from the Sun
Saturday Press
1983, 1990

Family Life
Story Line Press
1988, 1992

Getting Under Way: New and Selected Poems
Story Line Press
1993

Book design by Lysa McDowell

This book was set in Palatino type
using Aldus PageMaker 4.01 on a Machintosh computer

Book printing by McNaughton & Gunn